First World War
and Army of Occupation
War Diary
France, Belgium and Germany

32 DIVISION
97 Infantry Brigade,
Brigade Trench Mortar Battery
1 July 1916 - 31 August 1916

WO95/2404/5

The Naval & Military Press Ltd
www.nmarchive.com
Published in association with The National Archives

Published by

The Naval & Military Press Ltd

Unit 10 Ridgewood Industrial Park,

Uckfield, East Sussex,

TN22 5QE England

Tel: +44 (0) 1825 749494

www.naval-military-press.com

www.nmarchive.com

This diary has been reprinted in facsimile from the original. Any imperfections are inevitably reproduced and the quality may fall short of modern type and cartographic standards.

© **Crown Copyright**
Images reproduced by permission of The National Archives, London, England, 2015.

Contents

Document type	Place/Title	Date From	Date To
Heading	WO95/2404/5		
Heading	32nd Division 97th Infy Bde 97th Trench Mortar Bty Jly-Aug 1916		
Heading	97th Brigade 32nd Division 97th Trench Mortar Battery July 1916		
Heading	War Diary Of 97th Trench Mortar Battery From July 1st-July 31st 1916 Volume I		
War Diary	Authville Sector	01/07/1916	01/07/1916
War Diary	Aveluy	03/07/1916	03/07/1916
War Diary	Contay	04/07/1916	04/07/1916
War Diary	Harponville	05/07/1916	06/07/1916
War Diary	Senlis	07/07/1916	13/07/1916
War Diary	Ovillers Authville Wood Sector	14/07/1916	14/07/1916
War Diary	Bouzincourt	15/07/1916	15/07/1916
War Diary	Ampliers Sus St Leger	16/07/1916	18/07/1916
War Diary	Ocoche	19/09/1916	19/09/1916
War Diary	Huclier	20/07/1916	20/07/1916
War Diary	Allouagne	21/07/1916	25/07/1916
War Diary	Bethune	26/07/1916	31/07/1916
Heading	97th Brigade 32nd Division 97th Trench Mortar Battery August 1916		
Heading	War Diary Of 97th Trench Mortar Battery From August 1st-August 31st. 1916 Volume II		
War Diary	Bethune	01/08/1916	04/08/1916
War Diary	Annequin	05/08/1916	09/08/1916
War Diary	Cambrin	10/08/1916	20/08/1916
War Diary	Bethune	21/08/1916	22/08/1916
War Diary	Philosophe	23/08/1916	29/08/1916
War Diary	Bethune	30/08/1916	31/08/1916

WO 95/24045

32ND DIVISION
97TH INFY BDE

97TH TRENCH MORTAR BTY

JLY - AUG 1916

97th Brigade.

32nd Division.

97th TRENCH MORTAR BATTERY

JULY 1916

Vol I

Confidential

War Diary of
9n/7th Trench Mortar Battery
from July 1st – July 31st, 1916.
Volume I.

97th T.M. BATTERY

WAR DIARY

Army Form C. 2118

Place	Date	Hour	Summary of Events and Information	Remarks and references to Appendices
AUTHUILLE SECTOR	1/7/16		Preparatory to the assault the Battery fired rapid on the enemy's front line ceasing fire as the attacking Infantry advanced. The 4 guns in the night appear to have reached the enemy's lines but owing to lack of ammunition were of little use, the carrying party having failed to keep up the supply. Both 2/Lt. T. MIDDLETON and 2/Lt. J.K.C. BROWNLIE casualties. The 4 left guns finding that the Infantry had failed to stand or getting in the enemy's line treated their guns, one line being held by a few remaining Infantry. 2/Lt V.M. McINTOSH was killed.	
AVELUY	3.7.16		Relieved by another Battery and billeted in AVELUY.	
CONTAY	4.7.16		Marched to CONTAY + went into billets.	
HARPON-VILLE	5.7.16		Marched to HARPONVILLE + billeted. 97th Bde supplying Transport.	
do	6.7.16		In billets at HARPONVILLE	
SENLIS	7.7.16		Marched to billets in SENLIS.	
	8.7.16		Took over T.M. emplacements in line running from AUTHUILLE WOOD to OVILLERS LA BOISSELLE. Half Battery remaining at CRUCIFIX CORNER.	
	9.7.16		Placed a third gun in this portion of the line. Very little firing indeed.	
	10.7.16		Relieved ammunition + placed it in gun positions	
	11.7.16		Placed a gun in line, making 4, 2 guns remaining in support.	
	12.7.16		Relieved the gun teams in line by exchanging those in support + at CRUCIFIX CORNER.	
	13.7.16		Fired a few rounds + built up a larger ammunition dump with support guns also target. Returned to base handed.	

Army Form C. 2118

WAR DIARY
or
INTELLIGENCE SUMMARY
(Erase heading not required.)

Instructions regarding War Diaries and Intelligence Summaries are contained in F.S. Regs., Part II. and the Staff Manual respectively. Title Pages will be prepared in manuscript.

Place	Date	Hour	Summary of Events and Information	Remarks and references to Appendices
OVILLERS – AUTHUILLE WOOD SECTOR	14.7.16		Fired a few rounds into enemy communication trench junctions.	(Initialed)
BOUZINCOURT	15.7.16		Relieved by another T.M. Bty. & proceeded to billets at BOUZINCOURT.	(Initialed)
AMPLIERS	16.7.16		Marched to AMPLIERS & billeted in huts. Weather very bad.	(Initialed)
SUS ST LEGER	17.7.16		G.O.C. 32nd Division inspected the Brigade. Marched to billets in SUS ST LEGER.	(Initialed)
do	18.7.16		Refitting etc.	(Initialed)
OCOCHE	19.7.16		Marched to billets in OCOCHE.	(Initialed)
HUCLIER	20.7.16		Marched to billets in HUCLIER.	(Initialed)
ALLOUAGNE	21.7.16		Marched to billets in ALLOUAGNE.	(Initialed)
	22.7.16		Gun drill & inspection.	(Initialed)
	23.7.16		2/Lt S.P. JACOBY and 1 O.R. reported for duty.	7.(Initialed)
	24.7.16		Drill etc. 1 O.R. to hospital sick.	2.(Initialed)
	25.7.16		do. 1 O.R. to hospital sick. 1 O.R. Retd to duty. Battery bathed & obtained clean clothing.	(Initialed)
BETHUNE	26.7.16		do. 1 O.R. to Hospital sick. 2 O.R. Retd to duty. Marched to billets in BETHUNE.	(Initialed)
	27.7.16		Drill etc. Bathing Parade at Swimming baths.	(Initialed)
	28.7.16		do. 1 O.R. to hospital sick. 1 O.R. retd to duty.	(Initialed)
	29.7.16		Route March followed by bathing parade.	(Initialed)
	30.7.16		Drill etc. Firing practised with T.M's. 1 O.R. to hospital.	(Initialed)
	31.7.16		Drill etc. Bathing Parade at Swimming baths.	(Initialed)

Th. McDougall 2Lt.
97th T.M. Battery.

97th Brigade.

32nd Division.

97th TRENCH MORTAR BATTERY

AUGUST 1 9 1 6

Confidential.

War Diary of
97th Trench Mortar Battery.
from August 1st — August 31st, 1916.
Volume II.

Vol 2

9th T.M. BATTERY

WAR DIARY
INTELLIGENCE SUMMARY

Army Form C. 2118

Place	Date	Hour	Summary of Events and Information	Remarks and references to Appendices
BETHUNE.	1/8/16		Gun Drill + bombing also Physical Exer.	(APM) (APM)
	2.8.16		ditto. 1 O.R. to hospital sick.	(APM)
	3.8.16		ditto. O.C. Battery proceeded to view the CAMBRIN Sector	(APM)
	4.8.16		Gun Drill, Battery Parade.	
ANNEQUIN	5.8.16		Marched to ANNEQUIN + took over from 9 24th T.M. Bty. Half the Bty. went into the line + the other half billeted in billets at ANNEQUIN. 2 Lt. g. M. Benton and 2 Lt. J.H. SIMCOCK and 4 O.R. reported for duty.	(APM)
	6.8.16		Searched places for alternative T.M. positions, began making to retaliation.	(APM) (APM)
	7.8.16		Started work on 2 new emplacements. Retaliated to enemy fire.	(APM)
	8.8.16		Fired a great deal on enemy line. Work continued in emplacements.	(APM)
	9.8.16		Placed 2 guns with 2mos and 200 bombs in VILLAGE LINE for use in counter attack.	(APM)
CAMBRIN	10.8.16		1 O.R. to hospital sick. Fired in enemy trench junctions. Battery Hqrs moved to FACTORY TRENCH	(APM)
	11.8.16		The usual T.M. activity during the night. Carried on with work on new emplacements.	(APM)
	12.8.16		1 O.R. evacuated to No. 1 C.C.S. CHOQUES. 1 O.R. to hospital. 1 O.R. retd. to duty.	(APM)
	13.8.16		1 O.R. retd. to duty; a T.M. bombardment of the enemy lines took place in the afternoon.	(APM)
	14.8.16		2 Lt HULLEN H. reported for duty. Work on new emplacements proceeded with.	(APM)
	15.8.16		Retaliated effectively for enemy T.M. activity.	(APM)
	16.8.16	3 P.M.	Carried out a bombardment of enemy trench junctions etc.	(APM)
	17.8.16	5 P.M.	1 O.R. to hospital sick. Bombarded enemy front line.	(APM)
	18.8.16		Work on emplacements continued. a good deal of firing was necessary to silence enemy T.M.s.	(APM)
	19.8.16 9 P.M.		Only a counter attack position near ARTHUR'S KEEP.	(APM)
	20.8.16	5 P.M.	Walk on emplacements + bomb stores. Carried out a hurricane bombardment for 20 minutes.	(APM)
BETHUNE.	21.8.16		Relieved in this sector by 96th T.M. Bty. Marched to billets in BETHUNE	(APM)

WAR DIARY / INTELLIGENCE SUMMARY

Army Form C. 2118

Place	Date	Hour	Summary of Events and Information	Remarks and references to Appendices
BETHUNE.	22.8.16		Cleaned up guns & overhauled all stores. Battery stands for battery.	ZMW
PHILOSOPHE	23.8.16	9a.m.	Left BETHUNE and took over the light T.M. positions of the 48th T.M.B. in HULLUCH SECTOR. Left the Battery billets in PHILOSOPHE.	ZMW
	24.8.16		Retaliated for two T.M. bombs. Carried up more ammunition. Firing & retaliating.	ZMW
	25.8.16		Carried up ammunition from Bde stores to guns.	ZMW
	26.8.16		2/LT SPJAGOBY to hospital sick. 2/LT MULLEN relieved this officer in the trenches. 1 O.R. sick hospital.	ZMW
	27.8.16		Gun teams in line relieved by 2 gun teams with counter attack guns & teams in PHILOSOPHE. 2 teams from the line taking over counter attack guns & teams withdrawn to PHILOSOPHE.	ZMW
	28.8.16		Work carried out on emplacements.	ZMW
	29.8.16	4:20 p.m.	Heavily bombarded enemy's sap behind the craters in HULLUCH SECTOR till 4.50 p.m. with an interval of 10 minutes. A heavy thunderstorm bombardment & flooded our trenches lying over this sector during the	ZMW
BETHUNE.	30.8.16	7 p.m.	Relieved by 6th T.M. Bty who took over our gun positions etc. The Battery Retired to billets in BETHUNE.	ZMW
	31.8.16	1:30 p.m.	Battery paraded for battles.	ZMW

Th. Th. Dougall Lt
97th T.M. Bty

www.ingramcontent.com/pod-product-compliance
Lightning Source LLC
Chambersburg PA
CBHW051529190426
43193CB00045BA/2672